Provincial and Territorial Governments

by Anita Yasuda

Weigl

Published by Weigl Educational Publishers Limited
6325 10th Street S.E.
Calgary, AB T2H 2Z9
Website: www.weigl.com

All of the Internet URLs given in the book were valid at the time of publication.
However, due to the dynamic nature of the Internet, some addresses may have
changed, or sites may have ceased to exist since publication. While the author and
publisher regret any inconvenience this may cause readers, no responsibility for any
such changes can be accepted by either the author or the publisher.

Library and Archives Canada Cataloguing-in-Publication Data available upon request.
Fax (403) 233-7769 WEIGL for the attention of the Publishing Records department.

ISBN 978-1-55388-678-5 (hard cover)
ISBN 978-1-55388-682-2 (soft cover)

Printed in the United States of America in North Mankato, Minnesota
1 2 3 4 5 6 7 8 9 0 14 13 12 11 10

082010
WEP230610

Project Coordinator: Heather C. Hudak
Project Editor: Amanda Hudson
Photo Research: Edward A. Thomas
Design: Tammy West

Every reasonable effort has been made to trace ownership and to obtain
permission to reprint copyright material. The publishers would be pleased
to have any errors or omissions brought to their attention so that they may
be corrected in subsequent printings.

Weigl acknowledges Getty Images as its primary image supplier for this title.

Photo of Supreme Court of Canada on page 15 is by Philippe Landreville.
Copyright © Supreme Court of Canada.

We gratefully acknowledge the financial support of the Government of Canada
through the Canada Book Fund for our publishing activities.

CONTENTS

Introduction to Canada's Government

Large groups of people need rules for each member to follow. Most countries, cities, and towns have a government for this purpose. Government also organizes large groups of people to accomplish things an individual could not do alone. Most governments, for example, make and enforce laws, collect taxes, construct roads and bridges, educate children, and provide for defence.

Many countries, such as Canada, have a democratic form of government. The words *democratic* and *democracy* come from the Greek words *demos*, or "people," and *kratos*, or "power." In other words, the people have power.

There are two forms of democracy: **direct democracy** and **representative democracy**. Direct democracy gives every citizen the right to vote on every issue. Athens and many other city-states in ancient Greece governed themselves in this way. Requiring citizens across a large country to gather, debate ideas, and vote on every issue is not practical, however.

Most democratic countries, including Canada, are representative democracies. Citizens elect representatives to attend meetings, vote on issues, and make laws for them. Each person has a voice in government by voting in elections. However, only a small group of representatives has the power to make decisions.

Canada has three levels of government. Each level of government has its own powers and responsibilities. The **federal** government controls matters common to all provinces and territories. Provincial and territorial governments handle matters that are unique to each province and territory. Municipal governments manage matters that affect individual cities, towns, villages, and other municipalities.

Saskatchewan's Legislative Assembly meets to discuss provincial issues in the Saskatchewan Legislative Building.

Think about it!

1. List three things your government does that you could not do alone.

2. Why do you think Canada is a representative rather than a direct democracy?

3. Can you think of some advantages and disadvantages of having a representative government?

What is a Provincial or Territorial Government?

One of Manitoba's best-known symbols, the Golden Boy, stands on top of the Legislative Building.

A provincial government is responsible for all the citizens of a province. Provincial governments make laws for and provide services to the people of their province. They are responsible for important services such as schools and hospitals.

Provincial government is the middle level of Canada's three levels of government. Above it is the federal government, which makes laws for the country as a whole. The federal government has the main responsibility for government activities that need to be the same nationwide. These include defence, foreign policy, and the postal service.

Below the provincial governments are municipal governments. Within each province, responsibility for such local matters as libraries, bus service, trash collection, and recycling rests largely with municipal governments.

Territorial governments are similar to provincial governments. The federal government, however, has more control over territories than provinces. Public land in the territories is federally owned. The federal government controls natural resources and taxes in the territories.

Provincial governments receive money from the federal government to help them pay for some of the services they provide and for other programs. Provincial governments also raise money by collecting property taxes and sales taxes from people in the province.

Powers and Responsibilities in Government

This list shows some of the powers and responsibilities that fall under each level of Canada's three levels of government. Some of these responsibilities are shared.

Federal Government

- taxation (direct and indirect)
- national defence
- regulation of trade and commerce
- foreign policy
- criminal law and procedure
- citizenship and immigration
- employment insurance
- money and banking
- patents and copyrights
- census and statistics
- Indian affairs and Northern development
- postal service

Provincial Government

- direct taxation in the province
- civil law
- provincial courts
- natural resources and environment
- hospitals
- provincial prisons
- social services
- education

The territorial governments (Yukon Territory, Northwest Territories, and Nunavut) have many of the same powers as the provinces. Their powers are not guaranteed by the **Constitution**, however.

Municipal Government

- electric utilities
- economic development
- water and sewage
- emergency services
- libraries
- public transit
- land-use planning
- waste collection and recycling
- animal control

Provincial and Territorial Government Structure

Canada has ten provinces and three territories. Each provincial or territorial government has three branches. They are the executive, legislative, and judicial branches. Having three branches ensures that no one branch has too much power. Each branch has a different role.

The structure of Canada's provincial and territorial governments is based on Great Britain's **parliamentary system**. Under this system, key members of the executive branch, such as the **premier** and the cabinet, are also members of the legislative branch.

A provincial or territorial legislature has one chamber in which the members meet.

Unlike Canada's federal Parliament, which has two houses, provincial and territorial legislatures have only one house, or **chamber**. Often, the legislature is called the **Legislative Assembly**. In some provinces, the legislature is called the National Assembly or House of Assembly. Each member is elected to the legislature from an electoral district within the province or territory. Districts are also called ridings, constituencies, or sometimes electoral divisions.

District boundaries are drawn so that each district has about the same number of people.

The legislative branch of a provincial government also includes the British monarch's representative in the province. This person is called the **lieutenant governor**. He or she is appointed by Canada's **governor general**. The lieutenant governor must approve all laws passed by a provincial legislature. This is called giving **royal assent**.

Each territorial government has a commissioner. This person is the federal government's representative in the territory. The commissioner's role is similar to a lieutenant governor's.

Provinces and Territories of Canada

PROVINCE	NAME OF LEGISLATURE	NUMBER OF MEMBERS
Alberta	Legislative Assembly	83
British Columbia	Legislative Assembly	85
Manitoba	Legislative Assembly	57
New Brunswick	Legislative Assembly	55
Newfoundland and Labrador	House of Assembly	48
Nova Scotia	House of Assembly	52
Ontario	Legislative Assembly	107
Prince Edward Island	Legislative Assembly	27
Quebec	National Assembly	125
Saskatchewan	Legislative Assembly	58
TERRITORY	**NAME OF LEGISLATURE**	**NUMBER OF MEMBERS**
Northwest Territories	Legislative Assembly	19
Nunavut	Legislative Assembly	19
Yukon Territory	Legislative Assembly	18

The Executive Branch

The premier is the head of a provincial government. Dalton McGuinty (far right) was elected premier of Ontario in 2003.

The executive branch includes the premier and the cabinet. The premier is the head of the provincial or territorial government. In most cases, he or she is the leader of the **political party** that has the most seats in the legislature. Each party chooses its party leader. In the Northwest Territories and Nunavut, where members of the legislature are not elected from political parties, all members of the legislature vote to choose the premier.

The premier directs the government with help from his or her cabinet. In some regions of Canada, the cabinet is also known as the Executive Council.

The premier chooses a cabinet from the elected members of the legislature. The cabinet members generally belong to the same political party as the premier. The size of the cabinet varies from region to region.

The premier usually tries to pick cabinet members, often called cabinet ministers, who come from districts in different parts of the province or territory. This way, the ideas and needs of people living in all parts of the region are represented in the cabinet.

The premier and cabinet meet often. They make decisions about what the provincial or territorial government does and about what new laws they want to ask the legislature to pass. Once the premier and cabinet make a decision about government policy, all cabinet ministers are expected to support it. If a minister is unable to support a cabinet decision, this person must step down.

The executive branch also includes the departments that perform different government functions, such as departments for education, finance, or agriculture. Usually, each cabinet minister is in charge of one government department. Cabinet ministers supervise the people who work in their department. These workers are called civil servants. Ministers are responsible for the actions of their department. They must report on their department's activities to the cabinet and the legislature.

The executive branch includes a department for education.

The Legislative Branch

Voting in general elections for members of a legislature usually takes place at polling stations. These stations are often located in schools.

The legislature writes, debates, and votes on **bills**. A bill is a proposed law. Bills are passed by a **majority** vote in the legislature. Once a bill has been passed and is approved by the lieutenant governor or territorial commissioner, it becomes a provincial or territorial law. Actions taken by a legislature affect the everyday lives of people in the province or territory.

Each legislature is made up of elected members. Elections must be held at least once every five years. The time between these elections may be shorter, though, if the premier calls for an election sooner.

Except in the Northwest Territories and Nunavut, most members of the legislature belong to a political party, such as the Liberal Party, the Conservative Party, the New Democratic Party, the Green Party, or the Bloc Québécois. Members who do not belong to a particular party are called **independents**.

Legislatures meet at certain times of the year to pass laws and debate government policy. At these times, the legislature is said to be "in session." Some provinces have fixed schedules. This means the legislative session opens on the same day every year. In all provinces and territories, members are expected to attend all meetings of the legislature during a session.

Canada's major political parties include the Conservative Party, the Bloc Québécois, the New Democratic Party, the Liberal Party, and the Green Party.

The Judicial Branch

The judicial branch of government includes the courts of the province or territory. Courts hear criminal cases. They deal with civil cases, such as disputes between people or companies. They can also make decisions about what a law means.

Except in Nunavut, where all cases are heard by the Nunavut Court of Justice, every province and territory has several different levels of courts. The number of levels can vary. Some provinces, such as Prince Edward Island, have only three levels of courts. Nova Scotia has five.

The Court of Appeal for Ontario is located in Osgoode Hall in downtown Toronto.

Often, the lowest level or levels of provincial and territorial courts will handle such matters as traffic cases or civil cases involving small amounts of money. These are called small claims cases. The lower-level courts may also deal with cases that involve child protection.

Each province also has superior courts. These courts generally handle more serious criminal or civil cases and family offences. Superior courts may also hear appeals of lower court decisions. When a case is appealed, the party that has lost asks a higher court to review the decision made in the lower court and decide whether the decision agrees with the law.

The Supreme Court of Canada is made up of nine judges.

The highest level of provincial court is the court of appeals. This court generally hears appeals in the most serious civil and criminal cases. These appeals are usually heard by a panel of three judges. The chief justice is the judge in charge of running the court of appeals. Some court of appeals decisions may be further appealed to the Supreme Court of Canada. A panel of three Supreme Court judges reviews the applications from people who want to appeal. These judges may receive up to 600 applications in a year. They accept about 80 of them.

The judges who serve in each court must listen to facts, interpret the law, and make a fair decision. Judges in the superior and appeals courts are appointed by the federal government. Judges in the lower courts are appointed by the provincial government. A judge can serve until she or he decides to retire or reaches the age of 75.

The Legislative Process

The legislative branch of government passes bills. A bill can be private or public. Public bills are usually introduced to the legislature by a cabinet minister. The minister who introduces the bill is the head of the department most affected. For example, the minister for education will introduce a bill about schools. The minister will often make a short speech explaining the main points of the bill. He or she states why the bill is an important part of the government's program, or plan, for how the province or territory should be run.

Bills are studied and debated before becoming law. All members of the legislature can participate in debates. A bill is read three times. During the second and third readings, it may be changed, and it is voted on. Since the government often has a majority of seats in the legislature, bills introduced by a cabinet minister are generally passed. The bill must then receive approval from the lieutenant governor or territorial commissioner.

Bills about schools are introduced by the minister for education.

A private bill can be brought before the legislature by any member. Private bills are less common than public bills and usually affect only a single person or company. They do not come from cabinet ministers.

Public bills can also be introduced as a private member's bill. This type of bill is introduced by any member and not by a cabinet minister. It is intended to bring a certain issue to the attention of the legislature and the public. Private member's bills rarely pass, but they are often used to push the government toward taking some type of action.

How a Bill is Passed to Become Law

For a bill to pass, it must move through three stages, called "readings," in a legislature. Before a public bill is introduced, members must be given written notice 48 hours in advance. They must be told the name of the bill.

The First Reading
- The bill's title is announced.
- The minister responsible for the bill may make a speech explaining its purpose.
- At the First Reading there is no debate, and no changes may be made to the text.
- Members will study the bill.
- The bill is sent to be printed and distributed.

The Second Reading
- The bill is presented to the legislature for debate.
- The minister responsible for the bill may make a speech explaining the bill.
- Members debate the principle of the bill. A member may make only one speech.
- The minister responsible for the bill may make a closing speech.
- The bill is voted on. If the bill passes, it goes to a committee.
- The committee will examine the bill.

The Third Reading
- The bill is presented to the legislature for final debate.
- No changes to the bill are allowed at this stage.
- Members vote on the bill.

In Force
- The bill is now law.
- Many bills go into effect immediately. Some do not take effect until a later date.

Royal Assent
- If the bill passes, it is presented to the lieutenant governor or territorial commissioner.
- The lieutenant governor approves the bill on behalf of the British monarch, or the commissioner approves it on behalf of the federal government.

Graydon Nicholas, shown here with his wife and Queen Elizabeth II, became lieutenant governor of New Brunswick in 2009. A bill must be approved by the lieutenant governor or territorial commissioner.

Key People in Provincial and Territorial Government

The British North America Act of 1867, now called the Constitution Act, 1867, united Canada under one federal government. It allowed each province to keep its own legislature. There are different types of officials in the legislative branch of a provincial or territorial government.

Members of the Legislature

In most provinces and territories, the legislature is called the Legislative Assembly. In these places, citizens elected to the legislature are often called Members of the Legislative Assembly, or MLAs. In some provinces, other names are used. A member represents the people of his or her riding. He or she must also think about the interests of the whole province.

The Constitution Act, 1867, allowed each province to keep its own legislature.

The Speaker

The Speaker is a member of the legislature who oversees the proceedings in the chamber. This person is elected in a secret **ballot** by all MLAs. The Speaker makes certain that all points of view are heard during debates and question periods. The question period is a set amount of time when members may question ministers about government actions and policies. The Speaker does not take part in debates and votes only to break a tie.

The Lieutenant Governor

The lieutenant governor of a province represents the British monarch in that province. This person is named by the governor general and serves for a period of five years. At the opening of every new session, the lieutenant governor reads the **Speech from the Throne**. This speech explains the government's goals. Other responsibilities include swearing in members of the cabinet, giving royal assent to bills, and closing the legislature when an election is called.

The Commissioner

Canada's three territories do not have a lieutenant governor. Each has a commissioner, who represents the federal government in the territory. A territory's commissioner has many of the same functions as a lieutenant governor.

The Premier

A premier is the leader of a province or territory. Premiers are not directly elected by all the people in that province or territory. Generally, the leader of the party that wins the largest number of seats in the legislature during an election becomes the premier. The premier then chooses the cabinet. When the premier's party has a majority of seats, which is called a majority government, the premier and cabinet can control which bills are passed in a legislature.

The Cabinet

Members of the cabinet help the premier make government decisions. In some provinces, the cabinet is known as the Executive Council. Cabinet ministers run government departments, propose new laws, and oversee the work of the civil service. They are responsible to the legislature for the activities of their department.

The Official Opposition

Opposite the premier is the leader of the official opposition. The opposition leader generally heads the party with the second-highest number of seats. The opposition often has different ideas from the ruling party's about government policy. Some opposition members will be asked by the opposition leader to be critics of specific government departments.

Legislative Buildings

The building in which a legislature meets is the provincial or territorial seat of government. It is located in the province or territory's capital city. The Nova Scotia House of Assembly, for example, meets in Province House in Halifax. Used since 1819, Province House is Canada's oldest legislative building.

Each legislative building has a chamber in which the elected members meet to debate, make speeches, and make decisions. Generally, the chamber has seats on two sides, divided by an

Visitors to Halifax may take free tours of Province House, Canada's oldest legislative building.

aisle. Seats on one side are for the party in power. Cabinet ministers sit in the front. Government members who are not in the cabinet sit behind the cabinet ministers. Seats in the opposite side of the chamber are for the opposition.

The public is allowed to watch proceedings in the chamber from a public gallery. Here, they can listen to debates. The gallery is divided into sections. There are areas for the media, for the public, and for guests of members of the legislature.

Each legislature has its own daily routine. In the province of Alberta's Legislative Assembly, for example, the day begins with the Speaker's procession. The Sergeant-at-Arms leads the way bearing the Mace. The Mace is a staff that is a symbol of the Speaker's authority. The Sergeant-at-Arms enters the chamber and calls, "Order, order! Mr. (or Madam) Speaker." Then, the Sergeant-at-Arms followed by the Speaker walk down the chamber's aisle, and the Speaker takes the chair at the head of the chamber.

The 85 members of British Columbia's Legislative Assembly meet in the Parliament Building in Victoria.

The Election Process

Elections give people a chance to voice their opinion. They must be held at least every five years. Usually, the time between elections is four years or less. The premier can ask for, or call, an election. In most cases, governments call an election at a point near the end of their term or when their popularity is high.

An election can also occur if the government loses an important vote in the legislature. This is called a vote of non-confidence. The premier then has to either resign or call an election.

Provincial laws control elections at the provincial level. Elections are run by a provincial **chief electoral officer**. This person organizes the election. His or her job includes hiring a staff to work during the election and making sure the ballots are ready. The chief electoral officer selects a **returning officer** for each riding to oversee the election in that district.

Generally, anyone who is eligible to vote can run for a seat in the legislature. To be a candidate, a person must be a Canadian citizen who is at least 18 years old on polling day. He or she must also be a resident of the particular province or territory holding the election.

Candidates campaign for votes. They give speeches and put up signs. The goal is to show voters why they are the best person for the job. Before people cast their vote, they learn about the candidates and the issues. They decide which candidate they think will best represent them in the legislature.

Jean Charest became premier of Quebec in 2003.

Voting most often takes place at polling stations. This chart shows the steps in the process of voting.

1. Confirm that your name appears on the voter list. If you are not on the voter list, you can register during a 28-day period before the election, at an advance polling station, or at a polling station on election day. You may also choose to vote during the advance polls or by special mail-in ballot.

2. You will receive a voter information card with the address of your polling station. If you do not receive a voter information card, call the returning officer in your electoral district.

3. Next, you will go to your polling station on election day. After showing proof of your identity and address, you will get a ballot paper.

4. At the polling station, you will vote by secret ballot in a private polling booth. To vote, you need to make a clear mark in the box by the name of the candidate you prefer.

5. Once you have voted, you will give your ballot to a polling station official. That person will put it into a ballot box.

6. The paper ballots are counted after the polls close.

7. The official results of the count are announced to the public.

Facts to Know

The legislature for each province and territory meets in its capital city. The map below shows the location of all provincial and territorial capitals, as well as the federal capital, Ottawa.

N

Yukon Territory
★ WHITEHORSE

Northwest Territories
★ YELLOWKNIFE

Nunavut

IQALUIT ★

Newfoundland and Labrador

ST JOHN'S ★

C A N A D A

British Columbia

Alberta
EDMONTON ★

VICTORIA ★

Saskatchewan
REGINA ★

Manitoba

WINNIPEG ★

Ontario

Quebec

QUEBEC ★

Prince Edward Island
★ CHARLOTTETOWN

FREDERICTON ★

New Brunswick

HALIFAX ★
Nova Scotia

OTTAWA ○

TORONTO ★

LEGEND
Federal capital ◎
Provincial or territorial capital ✪

Scale 0   300   600   900
                              Kilometres

Provincial Voter Statistics

A good voter turnout is very important. It is the best way for people to have a say in who governs them. Not everyone who is eligible to vote actually does, however. The table below shows voter turnout in Prince Edward Island elections from 1966 to 2007. What does this chart tell you about which elections had the highest and lowest voter turnouts?

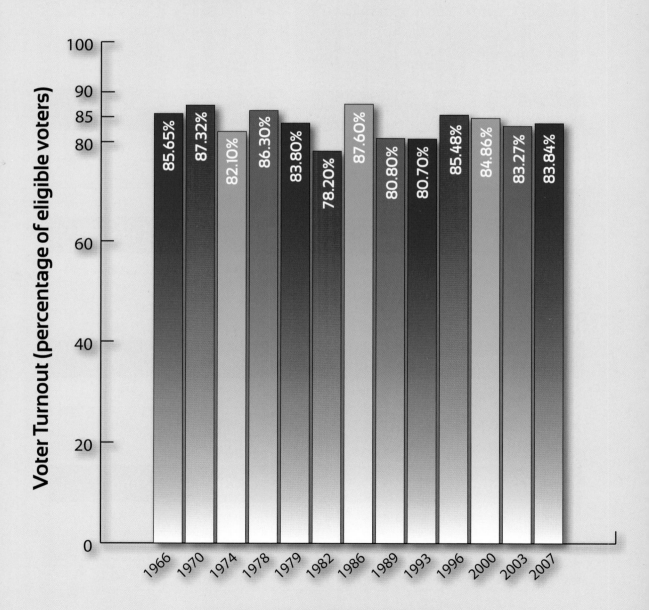

Voter Turnout by Age Group

Turnout among voters aged 18 to 24 is generally low across Canada. Some provinces are making efforts to encourage more people in this age group to vote. In British Columbia, Elections BC used Facebook.com and appointed a youth liaison officer to reach out to this age group. Look at the data in the table below from Statistics Canada. The numbers of voters are in thousands. What does the table tell you about voter turnout among 18-to-24-year-olds compared to other age groups?

Eligible Voters in All Age Groups	25,846	100 %
Voted in last federal election	18,809	72.8
Voted in last provincial election	18,662	72.2
Voted in last municipal election	15,201	58.8
Voters 18 to 24	**3,039**	**100 %**
Voted in last federal election	1,342	44.2
Voted in last provincial election	1,294	42.6
Voted in last municipal election	932	30.7
Voters 25 to 54	**14,625**	**100 %**
Voted in last federal election	10,326	70.6
Voted in last provincial election	10,195	69.7
Voted in last municipal election	8,008	54.8
Voters 55 and over	**8,181**	**100 %**
Voted in last federal election	7,140	87.3
Voted in last provincial election	7,173	87.7
Voted in last municipal election	6,261	76.5

Provincial Election Results

The chart below shows provincial election results from 1960 to 2010 for the province of New Brunswick. Twice in Canada's history there has been no official opposition after a provincial election. The first election was in Prince Edward Island in 1935. The second was in New Brunswick in 1987. Which political party won all 58 seats in New Brunswick's legislature in 1987?

YEAR OF ELECTION	SEATS WON				TOTAL NUMBER OF SEATS
	Liberal Party	New Democratic Party	Progressive Conservative Party	Other	
1960	31	-	21	-	52
1963	32	-	20	-	52
1967	32	-	26	-	58
1970	26	-	32	-	58
1974	25	-	33	-	58
1978	28	-	30	-	58
1982	18	1	39	-	58
1987	58	-	-	-	58
1991	46	1	3	8	58
1995	48	1	6	-	55
1999	10	1	44	-	55
2003	26	1	28	-	55
2006	29	-	26	-	55

Activities

Private Member's Bill

Any member of a legislature can propose a private member's bill. These bills rarely pass, but they are still important. Remember that they are often used to push the government toward taking some type of action. Imagine that you are creating a new private member's bill. This bill must be school related. Think about your topic. The topic might be school uniforms, school lunch, dismissal time, or funding for after-school activities. You must decide who your bill will benefit, as well as show why it is needed.

1. Give your bill a name. Come up with two or three possible titles that capture the spirit of your idea.

2. Outline what your bill will do and what its purpose is. Explain why your bill would have a positive impact.

3. Describe how you would make other members of the legislature aware of your bill.

4. Write down the steps involved in passing a bill. At what stage will your bill first be debated?

If the bill is passed, who would need to approve it in your province or territory?

Election Campaign Slogans

Campaign slogans tell people what a party or candidate stands for. Slogans are meant to be remembered. The goal is for people to hear the slogan and think of the candidate.

Here some examples of slogans used in provincial campaigns.

"A Better Plan"
–British Columbia Green Party, 2009

"It's Time"
–Alberta Liberal Party, 2008

"Now"
–Alberta Conservatives, 1971

"Masters in our own home"
–Quebec Liberals, 1962

Imagine that you and your friends or classmates work for a political campaign. You have been given the job of creating an election slogan.

1. Think of three slogans that would inspire people to vote for your candidate.

2. Create a 30-second radio commercial about your candidate that uses the slogan.

4. Design a campaign poster. The poster should use the slogan and explain what the candidate would do for the community.

5. Name places where you could put up your campaign posters.

6. Take a vote by secret ballot in your classroom or among your friends to choose the best slogan.

WHAT Have You LEARNED?

Answer these questions to see what you have learned about Canada's provincial and territorial governments.

1 Who is head of a provincial or territorial government?

2 What are the three branches of provincial and territorial government?

3 What is the highest provincial court?

4 Which level of government in Canada controls the postal service?

5 What is the name of Canada's oldest legislative building?

6 The member of the legislature who oversees the proceedings in the chamber is called what?

7 What happens if a cabinet minister is unable to support a cabinet decision?

8 How many provinces and how many territories are there in Canada?

9 Who does a lieutenant governor represent?

10 In most provinces and territories, what are the elected members of the legislature called?

ANSWERS: 1. A premier 2. Executive, legislative, and judicial 3. Court of appeals 4. The federal government 5. Province House, in Halifax 6. The Speaker 7. He or she must step down 8. 10 provinces and 3 territories 9. The British monarch 10. Members of the Legislative Assembly, or MLAs

Find Out More

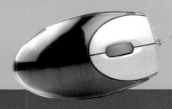

Many books and websites provide information on provincial and territorial governments. To learn more about provincial and territorial governments, borrow books from the library or do research online.

BOOKS

Most libraries have computers with an online catalog. If you input a key word, you will get a list of related books in the library. Nonfiction books are arranged numerically by call number. Fiction books are organized alphabetically by the author's last name.

WEBSITES

Libraries often have online reference databases that you can access from any computer. You can also use an Internet search engine, but be sure to verify the source of the website's information. Official websites run by government agencies are usually reliable, for example. To find out more about provincial or territorial governments, type key words, such as "Canada's system of provincial government," "Canada's provinces and territories," or the name of a Canadian province or territory, into the search field.

Words to Know

ballot: a ticket or sheet of paper used to cast a vote

bills: proposed laws

chamber: the room in which a legislative body meets

chief electoral officer: the person responsible for conducting provincial or territorial elections

constitution: the fundamental principles and rules under which a country is governed

direct democracy: a form of government that gives every citizen the right to vote on every issue

federal: national; usually used in reference to government

governor general: a representative appointed by the British monarch to represent him or her in Canada

independents: politicians who do not belong to a political party

Legislative Assembly: the most commonly used name for a provincial or territorial legislature

lieutenant governor: official who represents the British monarchy in a province

majority: more than half of a total

parliamentary system: a system of government in which the executive branch and the legislative branch work together

political party: a group of people who share similar ideas about how government should operate

premier: head of a provincial or territorial government

representative democracy: a form of government in which citizens do not take part directly but elect representatives to pass laws and make decisions on behalf of everyone

returning officer: the person in charge of the election in a particular riding

royal assent: the symbolic final stage of the legislative process by which a bill becomes a provincial law

Speech from the Throne: a speech read by the lieutenant governor at the opening of a new session of a legislature

INDEX